W9-CON-165

KEVIN DURANT

by **James Buckley Jr.**

Consultant: Ellen Labrecque
Former Editor and Writer
Sports Illustrated Kids

New York, New York

Credits
Cover, © Christopher Morris/ZUMA Wire/Alamy Live News; 4, © David E. Klutho/USA Today Sports; 5, © Xu Zijian/Xinhua News Agency/Newscom; 6, © Roy Dabner/EPA/Newscom; 7, © AP Photo/John Froschauer; 9, © Steve Boyle/Zuma Press/Newscom; 10, © AP Photo/Damian Dovarganes; 11, © Larry Smith/ICON SMI 769/Newscom; 12, © Greg Ashman/Icon SMI CCJ/Newscom; 13, © Jim Bryant/UPI/Newscom; 14, © Harry E. Walker/ABACAUSA.com/Newscom; 15, © AP Photo/Lynne Sladky; 16, © David E. Klutho/USA Today Sports; 18, © Fotoarena/SIPA USA/Newscom; 19, © Mathew Healy/UPI/Newscom; 20, © Larry W. Smith/EPA/Newscom; 21, © Jeff Siner/TNS/Newscom; 22L, © Mathew Healy/UPI/Newscom; 22R, © Lazyllama/Dreamstime; 22B, © Wouter Tolenaars/Dreamstime; 23, © David E. Klutho/USA Today Sports.

Publisher: Kenn Goin
Editor: Jessica Rudolph
Creative Director: Spencer Brinker
Production and Photo Research: Shoreline Publishing Group LLC

Library of Congress Cataloging-in-Publication Data

Names: Buckley, James, Jr., 1963–
Title: Kevin Durant / by James Buckley Jr.
Description: New York, New York : Bearport Publishing, 2018. | Series: Bearport's Library of Amazing Americans | Includes bibliographical references and index. | Audience: Age 5–8.
Identifiers: LCCN 2017005068 (print) | LCCN 2017009475 (ebook) | ISBN 9781684022427 (library) | ISBN 9781684022960 (ebook)
Subjects: LCSH: Durant, Kevin, 1988–Juvenile literature. | African American basketball players—Biography—Juvenile literature. | Basketball players—United States—Biography—Juvenile literature.
Classification: LCC GV884.D868 B83 2018 (print) | LCC GV884.D868 (ebook) | DDC 796.323092 [B] —dc23
LC record available at https://lccn.loc.gov/2017005068

For more information, write to Bearport Publishing Company, Inc., 45 West 21st Street, Suite 3B, New York, New York 10010. Printed in the United States of America.

10 9 8 7 6 5 4 3 2 1

CONTENTS

Going for Gold!

It was the 2016 Olympics. The U.S. men's basketball team was playing Serbia for the gold medal. The Americans led by just a few points, until Kevin Durant took over the game. He made a pair of three-point shots. Then he raced down the court for a slam dunk!

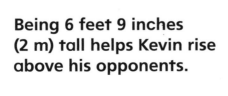

Being 6 feet 9 inches (2 m) tall helps Kevin rise above his opponents.

Kevin makes a slam dunk in the game against Serbia.

The 2016 Olympics were held in Rio de Janeiro, Brazil.

Early Champ

Kevin was born on September 29, 1988, in Washington, DC. He has loved basketball since he was a boy. Young Kevin played for a team called the Prince George Jaguars at a local sports club. When he was 11, his youth team won a national championship!

Kevin's Jaguars teammate, Michael Beasley, later played in the NBA, too.

Kevin's mother, Wanda, holds up his NBA jersey. Kevin wears number 35 to honor his youth coach, who died at age 35.

Growing Fast

By middle school, Kevin was already 6 feet (1.8 m) tall. He often played **guard**, even though that position is usually held by smaller players. Being a guard helped Kevin become better at dribbling, passing, and shooting the ball.

By his junior year of high school, Kevin had grown 8 inches (20 cm)! The following year, he started playing **forward**. His height and skill helped him become an **All-American**.

In 2013, Kevin gave $150,000 to sports clubs in the area where he grew up.

Kevin sits in the gym of his high school in Maryland.

A Longhorn

After high school, Kevin went to the University of Texas. In the 2006–2007 season, he helped his team win 25 games. He also averaged more than 25 points per game. Kevin won several awards, naming him the nation's best college basketball player.

Kevin won the 2007 John R. Wooden Award.

Kevin drives for the basket against the University of Oklahoma.

University of Texas sports teams are known as the Longhorns, which are a type of cow.

Young NBA Superstar

After Kevin played only one year of college ball, the Seattle SuperSonics chose him in the 2007 **NBA Draft**. The next year, his team moved to Oklahoma City and became the Thunder. Kevin was soon one of the NBA's best all-around players.

The Thunder was the first major pro sports team in Oklahoma.

In 2008, Kevin was named the NBA **Rookie** of the Year!

13

Better and Better

In 2012, Kevin led the Thunder to the NBA Finals, but his team lost to the Miami Heat. However, Kevin made the 2012 Olympic team. That summer, he headed to London, England. Kevin won his first Olympic gold medal when the U.S. team beat Spain in the final!

Kevin at the 2012 Olympics

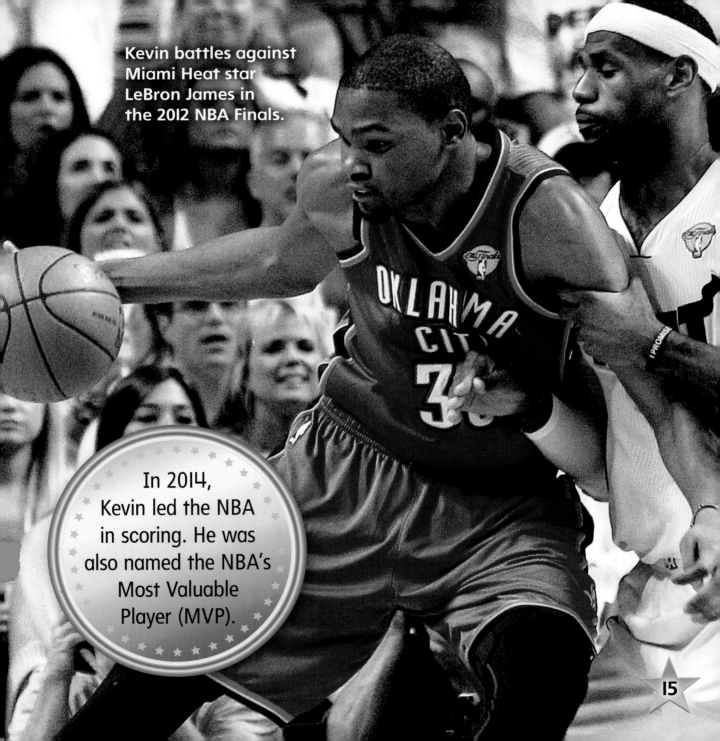

Kevin battles against Miami Heat star LeBron James in the 2012 NBA Finals.

In 2014, Kevin led the NBA in scoring. He was also named the NBA's Most Valuable Player (MVP).

On to Rio

At the 2016 Summer Olympics, Kevin joined 11 other NBA superstars in Rio. In the semifinals, Kevin scored 14 points against Spain, and the Americans won! The team moved on to the gold-medal game against Serbia.

In the semifinals, the United States beat Spain 82–76.

Kevin soars for a slam dunk.

Kevin holds the American flag at the 2016 Olympics.

Gold and Glory

At first, the game was close. By halftime, however, Kevin had earned 24 points. The entire Serbian team had scored only 29 points!

The final score was 96–66. The U.S. team had won! As the national anthem played, Kevin and his teammates proudly wore their gold medals.

Just two players on the 2012 Olympic team also played on the 2016 team—Kevin Durant and Carmelo Anthony.

Kevin Durant

Carmelo Anthony

A New Home

After the Olympics, Kevin joined the Golden State Warriors. The Warriors hope his all-around skills will help them win another title. If there is one thing Kevin is good at, it's winning!

Kevin has played in eight NBA All-Star Games.

Kevin helps make the Warriors a great team!

Timeline

Here are some key dates in Kevin Durant's life.

1980   1990   2000   2010   2020

September 29, 1988
Kevin Wayne Durant is born in Washington, DC.

2006
Named MVP of McDonald's All-American Game

2007
Chosen by Seattle SuperSonics in the NBA Draft

2008
SuperSonics move to Oklahoma City, become the Thunder

2010
Wins first of four scoring titles

2012
Wins first Olympic gold medal, in London

2016
Wins second Olympic gold medal, in Rio

2016
Joins the Golden State Warriors

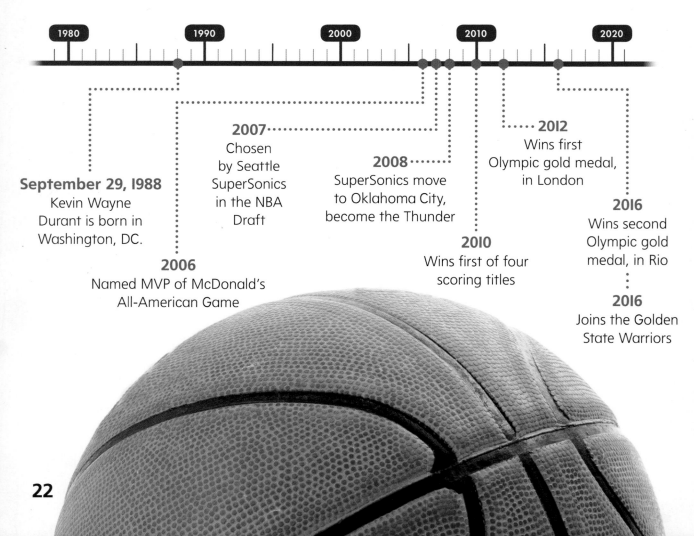

Glossary

All-American (AWL-uh-MARE-ih-kuhn) a high school or college athlete who is named one of the best at his or her position in the country

forward (FOR-wurd) a position usually played by taller players who score and gain possession of rebounds

guard (GARD) a position often played by shorter players who pass and dribble

NBA Draft (ENN-BEE-AY DRAFT) an event at which NBA teams pick new players

rookie (RUK-ee) a player in his or her first year of a pro sport

Index

Read More

Doeden, Matt. *Kevin Durant: Basketball Superstar.* North Mankato, MN: Capstone (2012).

Sandler, Michael. *Kevin Durant (Basketball Heroes Making a Difference).* New York: Bearport (2012).

Learn More Online

To learn more about Kevin Durant, visit
www.bearportpublishing.com/AmazingAmericans

About the Author

James Buckley Jr. has written dozens of books for young readers, mostly about sports.